Fun
Countries
Trivia Book
BY
CHUKU MICHAEL

Note from the Author
As this book ages, answers to some questions that are date-related and that are correct as of July 2022, and may likely change. However such questions are relatively small in number.

Disclaimer
I have done all the hard work to make sure that every answer contained in this book is correct and accurate. I however cannot accept responsibility for losses resulting from mistakes, errors, or omissions in this book. Please contact info@funsided.com if you discover an error or omission in this book.

TABLE OF CONTENT

60 Cities of the world Trivia Questions

1. Which country is the city of Bangkok located in?

2. Which country is the city of Dubai located in?

3. Which country is the city of Kuala Lumpur located in?

4. Which country is the city of Antalya located in?

5. Which country is the city of Shenzhen located in?

6. Which country is the city of Mumbai located in?

7. Which country is the city of Rome located in?

8. Which country is the city of Pattaya located in?

9. Which country is the city of Taipei located in?

10. Which country is the city of Mecca located in?

11. Which country is the city of Prague located in?

12. Which country is the city of Seoul located in?

13. Which country is the city of Amsterdam located in?

14. Which country is the city of Osaka located in?

15. Which country is the city of Barcelona located in?

16. Which country is the city of Milan located in?

17. Which country is the city of Vienna located in?

18. Which country is the city of Cancún located in?

19. Which country is the city of Orlando Lumpur located in?

20. Which country is the city of Venice located in?

21. Which country is the city of Ha Long located in?

22. Which country is the city of Toronto located in?

23. Which country is the city of Johannesburg located in?

24. Which country is the city of Sydney located in?

25. Which country is the city of Munich located in?

26. Which country is the city of Saint Petersburg located in?

27. Which country is the city of Brussels located in?

28. Which country is the city of Penang Island located in?

29. Which country is the city of Vancouver located in?

30. Which country is the city of Warsaw located in?

31. Which country is the city of Cebu City located in?

32. Which country is the city of Auckland located in?

33. Which country is the city of Tel Aviv located in?

34. Which country is the city of Nice located in?

35. Which country is the city of Porto located in?

36. Which country is the city of Rio de Janeiro located in?

37. Which country is the city of Zürich located in?

38. Which country is the city of Edinburgh located in?

39. Which country is the city of Cape Town located in?

40. Which country is the city of Geneva located in?

41. Which country is the city of Casablanca located in?

42. Which country is the city of Lagos located in?

43. Which country is the city of Accra located in?

44. Which country is the city of Kinshasa located in?

45. Which country is the city of Alexandria located in?

46. Which country is the city of Douala Lumpur located in?

47. Which country is the city of Kumasi located in?

48. Which country is the city of Kampala located in?

49. Which country is the city of Dakar located in?

50. Which country is the city of Freetown located in?

51. Which country is the city of Maputo located in?

52. Which country is the city of Cotonou located in?

53. Which country is the city of Dhaka located in?

54. Which country is the city of Wuhan located in?

55. Which country is the city of Baghdad Island located in?

56. Which country is the city of Riyadh located in?

57. Which country is the city of Salvador located in?

58. Which country is the city of Caracas located in?

59. Which country is the city of Cali located in?

60. Which country is the city of Valencia located in?

60 Language Trivia Questions

1. What is the official language of Albania?

2. What is the widely spoken language in Algeria?

3. What is the official language of Austria?

4. What is the official language of the Bahamas?

5. What is the official language of Barbados?

6. Is French an official language in Belgium?

7. Which is the largest Hindi-speaking country?

8. Which is the largest Spanish-speaking country?

9. Which is the largest English-speaking country in the world?

10. What is the official language of Brazil?

11. What is the official language of Bulgaria?

12. What is the official language of Colombia?

13. Which is the largest Portuguese-speaking country?

14. Which is the second largest Russian-speaking country?

15. Which is the largest Punjabi-speaking country?

16. Which is the largest Marathi-speaking country?

17. Which is the second largest Turkish-speaking country?

18. Which is the largest Korean-speaking country?

19. Which is the largest French-speaking African country?

20. Which is the second largest German-speaking country?

21. Which is the largest Javanese-speaking country?

22. Which is the second largest Italian-speaking country?

23. Which is the largest Arabic-speaking country?

24. Which is the largest Arabic-speaking Asian country?

25. Which is the largest Persian-speaking country?

26. Which is the largest English-speaking African country?

27. Which is the largest Spanish-speaking African country?

28. Which is the largest English-speaking Asian country?

29. Which is the largest Hausa-speaking country?

30. Which is the largest Polish-speaking country?

31. Which is the largest English speaking in Europe?

32. What is the second most spoken language in the United States?

33. What is the second most spoken language in Russia?

34. What is the 2nd most spoken language in the UK?

35. Which is the second largest Romanian-speaking country?

36. Which is the largest Kurdish-speaking country?

37. Which is the second largest Greek-speaking country?

38. Which country has the 2nd largest Spanish-speaking population in the world?

39. Which language is closest to Spanish?

40. Which is the largest Dutch-speaking country?

41. What is the official language of Costa Rica?

42. What is the official language of Cuba?

43. What is the official language of Denmark?

44. What is the official language of Dominica?

45. What is the official language of Egypt?

46. What is the official language of Gabon?

47. What is the official language of Grenada?

48. What is the official language of Guatemala?

49. What is the official language of Hungary?

50. What is the official language of Iceland?

51. What is the second official language of India aside from English?

52. What is the second official language of Finland aside from Finnish?

53. What is the official language of Georgia?

54. Which is the most popular unofficial language in Israel apart from English?

55. What is the official language of Madagascar aside from Malagasy?

56. What is the official language of Nigeria?

57. What is the official language of the Philippines aside from English?

58. What is the official language of Qatar?

59. What is the official language of Serbia?

60. Which of Tamil, English, Arabic, or Malay is not an official language of Singapore?

80 Countries Capitals Trivia

Questions

1. What is the capital of the United Arab Emirates?

2. Addis Ababa is the capital of which country?

3. Amsterdam is the official capital of which country?

4. What is the capital of Turkey?

5. What is the capital of Greece?

6. What is the capital of Iraq?

7. What is the capital of Thailand?

8. What is the capital of Lebanon?

9. What is the capital of China?

10. What is the capital of Germany?

11. What is the legislative capital of South Africa?

12. What is the capital of Brazil?

13. Bridgetown is the official capital of which country?

14. What is the capital of Belgium?

15. Budapest is the official capital of which country?

16. Buenos Aires is the official capital of which country?

17. What is the capital of Egypt?

18. Canberra is the official capital of which country?

19. What is the capital of Venezuela?

20. Colombo is the official capital of which country?

21. What is the capital of Denmark?

22. What is the capital of Senegal?

23. Damascus is the official capital of which country?

24. Dhaka is the official capital of which country?

25. Doha is the official capital of which country?

26. Dublin is the official capital of which country?

27. Freetown is the official capital of which country?

28. What is the capital of Ascension Island?

29. What is the capital of Guatemala?

30. What is the capital of Vietnam?

31. Havana is the official capital of which country?

32. What is the capital of Finland?

33. Islamabad is the official capital of which country?

34. What is the capital of Israel?

35. What is the capital of Afghanistan?

36. Kampala is the official capital of which country?

37. What is the capital of Indonesia?

38. What is the capital of Rwanda?

39. What is the capital of Jamaica?

40. What is the capital of Kuwait?

41. What is the capital of Ukraine?

42. Lima is the official capital of which country?

43. What is the capital of Portugal?

44. What is the capital of the United Kingdom?

45. Lusaka is the official capital of which country?

46. What is the capital of Luxembourg?

47. What is the capital of Spain?

48. Malé is the official capital of which country?

49. What is the capital of Mexico?

50. What is the capital of Belarus?

51. What is the capital of Monaco?

52. What is the capital of Russia?

53. Muscat is the official capital of which country?

54. What is the capital of Kenya?

55. What is the capital of India?

56. What is the capital of Norway?

57. What is the capital of Canada?

58. What is the capital of Panama?

59. What is the capital of France?

60. What is the capital of Mauritius?

61. What is the capital of Morocco?

62. What is the capital of Saudi Arabia?

63. What is the capital of Italy?

64. What is the capital of Costa Rica?

65. What is the capital of Puerto Rico?

66. What is the capital of South Korea?

67. What is the capital of Singapore?

68. What is the capital of Sweden?

69. What is the capital of Taiwan?

70. What is the capital of Iran?

71. What is the capital of Japan?

72. What is the capital of Tunisia?

73. What is the capital of Malta?

74. What is the capital of Seychelles?

75. What is the capital of Austria?

76. What is the capital of Poland?

77. What is the capital of New Zealand?

78. What is the capital of the United States?

79. What is the capital of Croatia?

80. What is the capital of Nigeria?

120 Currency Trivia Questions

1. What is the world's oldest currency still in use to date?

2. Which African currency has the highest value?

3. How much is a dime worth?

4. Which Asian currency has the highest value?

5. What is the weakest currency in Europe?

6. Which South American currency has the lowest Value?

7. Which South American currency has the highest value?

8. What is the currency code of the Afghanistan currency Afghani?

9. How many ATMs are in Antarctica?

10. What is the currency code of the Euro?

11. What is the currency code of the Indian Rupee?

12. Which country's dollar has the highest value apart from the USD?

13. What is the currency code of the Australian Dollar?

14. What is the currency code of the South African Rand?

15. What is the currency code of the New Zealand Dollar?

16. What is the currency code of the US Dollar?

17. What is the currency code of the Pound Sterling?

18. The Romans were the first ever to stamp the image of a living person on a coin in 44 B.C, whose image was first featured?

19. What is the official currency used in Algerian?

20. What is the official currency used in Argentine?

21. What is the official currency used in Australia?

22. What is the official currency used in Austria?

23. What is the official currency used in The Bahamas?

24. What is the official currency used in Bangladesh?

25. What is the currency code of Belarus currency, the Belarussian Ruble?

26. What is the official currency used in Belgium?

27. What is the official currency used in Bhutan?

28. What is the official currency used in Brazil?

29. What is the currency code of the Burundi currency, Burundi Franc?

30. What is the currency code of the Canadian Dollar?

31. What is the currency code of the East Caribbean Dollar?

32. In The United State, what is the most common paper denomination?

33. What is the currency code of CFA Franc BEAC used by countries like Chad and Cameroon?

34. What is the currency code of China currency Yuan Renminbi?

35. What other currency is used in Colombia apart from the Colombian Peso?

36. What is the official currency used in Costa Rica?

37. What is the official currency used in Croatia?

38. Who was the first American to be pictured on an American coin in 1909?

39. What other currency is used in Cuba apart from the Cuban Peso?

40. What is the official currency used in Denmark?

41. What is the official currency used in The Dominican Republic?

42. What is the official currency used in Ecuador?

43. What is the official currency used in Egypt?

44. What other currency is used in El Salvador apart from US Dollar?

45. What is the official currency used in Estonia?

46. What is the official currency used in Ethiopia?

47. What is the official currency used in Fiji?

48. What is the official currency used in Finland?

49. What is the official currency used in Germany?

50. What was the largest U.S. bill ever in circulation, which was issued in 1945?

51. What is the official currency used in Ghana?

52. What is the official currency used in Greenland?

53. What is the official currency used in Grenada?

54. What other currency is used in Haiti apart from US Dollar?

55. What is the official currency used in Hungary?

56. What is the official currency used in Hong Kong?

57. What is the official currency used in Iceland?

58. What is the most traded currency in the world?

59. What is the official currency used in India?

60. What is the official currency used in Indonesia?

61. What is the official currency used in Iran?

62. What is the official currency used in Ireland?

63. What is the official currency used in Israel?

64. What is the official currency used in Jamaica?

65. What is the currency code of the Japanese currency Yen?

66. What is the official currency used in Kenya?

67. What is the official currency used in Kuwait?

68. How many dollars are there in a grand?

69. What is the official currency used in South Korea?

70. What is the official currency used in Lebanon?

71. What is the official currency used in Libya?

72. What is the currency code of the Swiss Franc?

73. What is the official currency used in Malta?

74. What other currency is used in Mexico apart from Mexican Peso?

75. What is the official currency used in Morocco?

76. What is the official currency used in The Netherlands?

77. What is the official currency used in New Zealand?

78. What is the official currency used in Nigeria?

79. What is the official currency used in Norway?

80. What is the official currency used in Pakistan?

81. What other currency is used in Panama apart from US Dollar?

82. What is the official currency used in the Philippines?

83. What is the official currency used in Poland?

84. What is the official currency used in Portugal?

85. What is the official currency used in Qatar?

86. What is the currency code of the Russian Ruble?

87. What is the official currency used in Rwanda?

88. What is the official currency used in Serbia?

89. What is the official currency used in Singapore?

90. What is the official currency used in Slovakia?

91. What is the official currency used in South Africa?

92. What is the official currency used in Spain?

93. What is the official currency used in Sweden Krona?

94. What other currency is used in Switzerland apart from the Swiss Franc?

95. What is the official currency used in Syria?

96. What is the official currency used in Taiwan?

97. What is the official currency used in Thailand?

98. What is the official currency used in Turkey?

99. What is the official currency used in Ukraine?

100. What is the official currency used in the United Arab Emirates?

101. What is the official currency used in Venezuela?

102. What is the official currency used in Zimbabwe?

103. Which currency has the symbol R$?

104. Which currency has the symbol ¥?

105. Which currency has the symbol ₡?

106. Which currency has the symbol kn?

107. Which currency has the symbol ₱?

108. Which currency has the symbol CHF?

109. Which currency has the symbol RD$?

110. Which currency has the symbol €?

111. Which currency has the symbol ₺?

112. Which currency has the symbol Ft?

113. Which currency has the symbol ₹?

114. Which currency has the symbol ₱?

115. Which currency has the symbol ₪?

116. Which currency has the symbol J$?

117. Which currency has the symbol ₩?

118. Which currency has the symbol ₦?

119. Which currency has the symbol S/.?

120. Which currency has the symbol zł?

40 Airlines Trivia Questions

1. Which country owns Emirates Airline?

2. What is the national airline of the country of Qatar?

3. What is the national airline of the country of Saudi Arabia?

4. Which country owns AirAsia?

5. What is the national airline of the country of New Zealand?

6. Which country owns All Nippon Airways(ANA)?

7. Which country owns Asiana Airlines?

8. Which country owns Cathay Pacific?

9. Which country owns Cebu Pacific Air?

10. Which country owns China Airlines?

11. Which country owns Jet Airways?

12. Which country owns Jetstar?

13. Which country owns Kingfisher Airlines?

14. Which country owns Lion Air Airlines?

15. What is the national airline of the country of Malaysia?

16. What is the national airline of the United Kingdom?

17. Which country owns Delta Air Lines?

18. What is the national airline of Singapore?

19. Which country owns Virgin Blue Airlines?

20. Which country owns Aer Lingus?

21. What is the national airline of Russia?

22. What is the national airline of France?

23. Which country owns EasyJet?

24. Which country owns Lufthansa?

25. Which country owns the Norwegian Air Shuttle?

26. Which country owns Ryanair?

27. Which country owns Swiss?

28. What is the national airline of Turkey?

29. Which country owns Vueling Airlines?

30. What is the national airline of Canada?

31. Which country owns AirTran Airways?

32. Which country owns WestJet?

33. What is the national airline of Ethiopia?

34. What is the national airline of South Africa?

35. What is the national airline of Seychelles?

36. What is the national airline of Rwanda?

37. Which country owns Virgin Atlantic?

38. Which country owns KLM Royal Dutch Airlines?

39. Which country owns Finnair?

40. Which country owns Etihad Airways?

55 Brands Trivia Questions

1. What is the country of origin of Porsche?

2. What is the country of origin of Toyota?

3. What is the country of origin of Apple Inc?

4. What is the country of origin of Chanel?

5. What is the country of origin of GUCCI?

6. What is the country of origin of Nissan?

7. What is the country of origin of BMW?

8. What is the country of origin of Samsung Electronics?

9. What is the country of origin of Prada?

10. What is the country of origin of Louis Vuitton?

11. What is the country of origin of Bugatti?

12. What is the country of origin of Mercedes-Benz?

13. What is the country of origin of Cartier?

14. What is the country of origin of Ferrari?

15. What is the country of origin of Rolex?

16. What is the country of origin of Dior?

17. What is the country of origin of Estée Lauder?

18. What is the country of origin of Omega?

19. What is the country of origin of Burberry?

20. What is the country of origin of Ray-Ban?

21. What is the country of origin of SK-II?

22. What is the country of origin of Bentley?

23. What is the country of origin of Armani?

24. What is the country of origin of Givenchy?

25. What is the country of origin of Lamborghini?

26. What is the country of origin of Shangri-La?

27. What is the country of origin of Rolls- Royce?

28. What is the country of origin of Sulwhasoo?

29. What is the country of origin of Maserati?

30. What is the country of origin of Volkswagen?

31. What is the country of origin of Chevrolet?

32. What is the country of origin of GMC?

33. What is the country of origin of Ford?

34. What is the country of origin of Coca-Cola?

35. What is the country of origin of Red Bull?

36. What is the country of origin of Budweiser?

37. What is the country of origin of Heineken?

38. What is the country of origin of Volvo?

39. What is the country of origin of Huawei?

40. What is the country of origin of Dell Technologies?

41. What is the country of origin of Sony?

42. What is the country of origin of Panasonic?

43. What is the country of origin of Intel?

44. What is the country of origin of LG Electronics?

45. What is the country of origin of Fendi?

46. What is the country of origin of Hugo Boss?

47. What is the country of origin of Ralph Lauren?

48. What is the country of origin of Quaker Oats?

49. What is the country of origin of Maggi?

50. What is the country of origin of Green Giant?

51. What is the country of origin of Smirnoff?

52. What is the country of origin of Snickers?

53. What is the country of origin of Nescafé?

54. What is the country of origin of Pringles?

55. What is the country of origin of Heinz?

80 Countries slogan Trivia Questions

1. Which country is known as the breadbasket of Europe?

2. Which country is known as the holy land?

3. Which country is known as the land of volcanoes?

4. Which country is known as the Pompeii of Latin America?

5. What country is known as the land of windmills?

6. Which country's flag is known as the union jack?

7. Which country is also known as the land of the rising sun?

8. Which country is called the queen of sea?

9. Which country is called Yankee?

10. Which country is known as a white elephant?

11. Which country is known as the Amazon of Asia?

12. Which are countries called Asian tigers?

13. Which country is known as the "bowl of sugar of the world"?

14. In which country is the city of angels?

15. Which African country is the city of gold in?

16. Which country is known as the cockpit of Europe?

17. Which country is known as the coffee pot of the world?

18. Which country is known as the land of festivals?

19. Which country is known as the country of copper?

20. Which country is known as "the land of a thousand lakes"?

21. Which country is known as the land of rivers?

22. Which country is known as the country of winds?

23. Which country is known as Deutschland?

24. Which country is known as the diamond of the desert?

25. Which city is known as the eternal city?

26. Which country is known as emerald isle?

27. Which country is known as the giant of Africa?

28. Which country is known as the gift of Nile?

29. Which country is known as god's own country?

30. Which country is known as the gold coast?

31. Which country is known as the golden bird?

32. Which country is known as the graveyard of empires?

33. Which country is known as the heart of Asia?

34. Which country is known as heaven on earth?

35. Which country is known as the island of pearls?

36. Which country is known as the land of cakes?

37. Which country is known as the land of golden fiber?

38. Which country is known as the land of kangaroo?

39. Which country is known as the land of midnight sun?

40. Which country is known as the land of smiles?

41. Which country is known as the land of thunder?

42. Which country is known as little India?

43. Which country is known as the mistress of seas?

44. Which country is known as the pearl of the Indian ocean?

45. Which country is known as the pharmacy of the world?

46. Which country is known as the playground of Europe?

47. Which country is known as a rainbow nation?

48. Which country is known as the red dragon?

49. Which country is known as the rice bowl of the world?

50. Which country is known as the birthplace of democracy?

51. Which country is known as the hermit kingdom?

52. Which country is known as the land of golden fleece?

53. Which country is known as the land of morning calm?

54. Which country is known as the land of prophets?

55. Which country is known as the pearl of Africa?

56. Which country is known as Uncle Sam?

57. Which country is known as White Russia?

58. Which country is known as the workshop of the world?

59. Which country is known as the Land of Fire and Ice?

60. Which country is known as the Land of the Eagles?

61. Which country is known as The Land of Roses?

62. Which city is known as The land of a thousand islands?

63. Which country is known as The Land of Poets and Thinkers?

64. Which country is known as The Boot?

65. Which country is known as Billionaires' Playground?

66. Which country is known as Black Mountain?

67. Which country is known as The Sunny Side of the Alps?

68. Which country is known as The Emerald of the Equator?

69. Which country is known as The Pearl of the Orient Seas?

70. Which country is known as The Land of the Two Holy Mosques?

71. Which country is known as The Land of Four Seasons?

72. Which country is known as The Gulf Tiger?

73. Which country is known as The Great White North?

74. Which country is known as the melting pot?

75. Which country is known as the land of the Free?

76. Which country is known as The Gateway to South America?

77. Which country is known as the Land of Grace?

78. Which country is known as the Land of the Long White Cloud?

79. Which country is known as The Kingdom In the Sky?

80. Which country is known as the Land of the Upright Men?

30 Countries Motto Trivia Questions

1. What is the official motto of Brazil?

2. What is the official motto of Colombia?

3. What is the official motto of Canada?

4. What is the official motto of Cuba?

5. What is the official motto of the Democratic Republic of Congo?

6. What is the official motto of Denmark?

7. What is the official motto of the Dominican Republic?

8. What is the official motto of Europe?

9. Which country has the official motto of "Liberty, equality, fraternity"?

10. What is the official motto of Germany?

11. What is the official motto of Greece?

12. What is the official motto of Haiti?

13. What is the official motto of Hungary?

14. What is the official motto of India?

15. What is the official motto of Iran?

16. What is the official motto of Ireland?

17. What is the official motto of Jamaica?

18. What is the official motto of Malta?

19. What is the official motto of Mexico?

20. What is the official motto of Morocco?

21. What is the official motto of the Netherlands?

22. What is the official motto of New Zealand?

23. What is the official motto of Nigeria?

24. What is the official motto of Norway?

25. What is the official motto of Pakistan?

26. What is the official motto of Poland?

27. What is the official motto of Saudi Arabia?

28. What is the official motto of Spain?

29. What is the official motto of Switzerland?

30. What is the official motto of United Kingdom?

85 Citizens Trivia Questions

1. Citizens of Finland are called Finnish, what is a person from Finland called?

2. What are citizens of Australia called?

3. What is a person from Bangladesh called?

4. What are citizens of Belarus called?

5. Which Country's Citizens are called Belgians?

6. Citizens of Botswana are called Botswanans, what is a person from Botswana called?

7. Citizens of Britain are called British, what is a person from Britain called?

8. What are citizens of Brazil called?

9. What are citizens of Canada called?

10. What are citizens of China called?

11. What are citizens of Chile called?

12. Which Country's Citizens are called Congolese?

13. Which Country's Citizens are called Croat?

14. What are citizens of Cuba called?

15. Which Country's Citizens are called Cypriot?

16. What are citizens of the Czech Republic called?

17. Citizens of Denmark are called Danish, what is a person from Denmark called?

18. What are citizens of Ecuador called?

19. What are citizens of El Salvador called?

20. Which Country's Citizens are called Egyptians?

21. What are citizens of Ethiopia called?

22. Citizens of France are called French, what is a woman from France called?

23. What are citizens of Gabon called?

24. What are citizens of Georgia called?

25. What are citizens of Germany called?

26. What are citizens of Ghana called?

27. What are citizens of Greece called?

28. What is a person from Haiti called?

29. What are citizens of the Netherlands called?

30. What are citizens of Hungary called?

31. Citizens of Iceland are called Icelandic, what is a person from Iceland called?

32. What are citizens of India called?

33. What are citizens of Indonesia called?

34. What are citizens of Iraq called?

35. Citizens of Ireland are called Irish, what is a person from Ireland called?

36. What are citizens of Israel called?

37. What are citizens of Italy called?

38. What are citizens of Jamaica called?

39. What are citizens of Japan called?

40. What are citizens of Kazakhstan called?

41. What are citizens of Kuwait called?

42. What are citizens of Lebanon called?

43. What is a person from Luxembourg called?

44. What are citizens of Kuwait called?

45. A citizen of Madagascar is called a Madagascan or what?

46. What are citizens of Malaysia called?

47. What are citizens of Malta called?

48. What are citizens of Mexico called?

49. A citizen of Monaco is called a Monacan or what?

50. What are citizens of Mozambique called?

51. What are citizens of Nepal called?

52. A woman of the Netherland is called a Dutchwoman or what?

53. Citizens of which country are called Kiwis?

54. People from Nigeria are called Nigerian, what are people from Niger called?

55. What are citizens of North Korea called?

56. What are citizens of Norway called?

57. What are citizens of Pakistan called?

58. What are citizens of Peru called?

59. A person from the Philippines is called what?

60. People from Poland are called Polish, what is a person from Poland called?

61. What are citizens of Portugal called?

62. What are citizens of Qatar called?

63. What are citizens of Russia called?

64. A citizen of Saudi Arabia is called Saudi Arabian or what?

65. People from Scotland are called Scottish what is a person from Scotland called?

66. What are citizens of Senegal called?

67. A citizen of Serbia is called a Serbian or what?

68. What are citizens of Seychelles called?

69. What are citizens of Singapore called?

70. What are citizens of Slovakia called?

71. A citizen of Slovenia is called a Slovenian or what?

72. People from Spain are called Spanish what is a person from Spain called?

73. What are citizens of Sudan called?

74. People from Sweden are called Swedish what is a person from Sweden called?

75. What are citizens of Switzerland called?

76. People from Taiwan are called what?

77. What are citizens of Thailand called?

78. What are citizens of Togo called?

79. People from Turkey are called Turkish what is a person from Turkey called?

80. What is Ukraine of Togo called?

81. What are citizens of the United Arab Emirates called?

82. People from the United States of America are called Americans what is a person from the United States of America called?

83. What are citizens of Vietnam called?

84. What are people from Wales called?

85. What are citizens of Yemen called?

86. What is the official motto of the United Kingdom?

108 Countries Landmarks

Trivia Questions

1. Where is the statue of liberty located?

2. Where is Eiffel Tower located?

3. The Great Wall is located in which country?

4. Kremlin is located in which country?

5. St Basil's Cathedral is located in which country?

6. Mecca is located in which country?

7. Leaning Tower of Pisa is located in which country?

8. The Great Pyramid of Giza is located in which country?

9. Sydney Opera House is located in which country?

10. Taj Mahal is located in which country?

11. Machu Picchu is located in which country?

12. Big Ben is located in which country?

13. Colosseum is located in which country?

14. Empire State Building is located in which country?

15. Golden Gate Bridge is located in which country?

16. Tokyo Tower is located in which country?

17. St. Peter's Basilica is located in which country?

18. Arc de Triomphe is located in which country?

19. Berlin Wall is located in which country?

20. Stonehenge is located in which country?

21. Kilimanjaro is located in which country?

22. Uluru - Ayers Rock is located in which country?

23. The Great Sphinx Rock is located in which country?

24. Tower Bridge Rock is located in which country?

25. The Forbidden City is located in which country?

26. Mount Everest is located between which countries?

27. Willis Tower is located in which country?

28. Burj Al Arab Hotel is located in which country?

29. Acropolis is located in which country?

30. St. Mark's Campanile is located in which country?

31. Times Square is located in which country?

32. Buckingham Palace is located in which country?

33. The Palace of Versailles is located in which country?

34. Neuschwanstein Castle is located in which country?

35. Matterhorn Mountain is located in which country?

36. Pompeii is located in which country?

37. Florence Cathedral is located in which country?

38. Edinburgh Castle is located in which country?

39. Machu Picchu is located in which country?

40. CN Tower is located in which country?

41. The Grand Canyon is located in which country?

42. Niagara Falls is located between which countries?

43. Burj Khalifa is located in which country?

44. Mont St. Michel is located in which country?

45. Las Vegas is located in which country?

46. Petronas Twin Towers is located in which country?

47. Windsor Castle is located in which country?

48. Mount Rushmore is located in which country?

49. Mount Fuji is located in which country?

50. Rialto Bridge is located in which country?

51. Arena Di Verona is located in which country?

52. Space Needle is located in which country?

53. Rock of Gibraltar is located in which country?

54. Alcatraz is located in which country?

55. Washington Monument is located in which country?

56. The Shard is located in which country?

57. The Gherkin is located in which country?

58. Temple of Luxor is located in which country?

59. Brandenburg Gate is located in which country?

60. Pentagon is located in which country?

61. Mount Vesuvius is located in which country?

62. Mayan Pyramids of Chichen Itza is located in which country?

63. Victoria Falls is located between which countries?

64. Terracotta Warriors is located in which country?

65. Potala Palace is located in which country?

66. Oriental Pearl Tower is located in which country?

67. Ponte Vecchio is located in which country?

68. Wailing Wall is located in which country?

69. Summer Palace is located in which country?

70. Mount Etna is located in which country?

71. Great Buddha is located in which country?

72. Freedom Tower is located in which country?

73. Moulin Rouge is located in which country?

74. Mill Complex at Kinderdijk is located in which country?

75. Catherine Palace in which country?

76. Helsinki Cathedral is located in which country?

77. Tivoli Gardens is located in which country?

78. Giant's Causeway is located in which country?

79. Papal Palace, Avignon is located in which country?

80. Table Mountain is located in which country?

81. Winter Palace is located in which country?

82. Death Valley is located in which country?

83. Blue Mosque is located in which country?

84. Statue of Unity is located in which country?

85. Lake Hillier is located in which country?

86. The Harbor of Rio de Janeiro is located in which country?

87. Grand Canyon is located in which country?

88. Milford Sound is located in which country?

89. Great Barrier Reef is located in which country?

90. What is the name of the rain forest that touched BRAZIL, PERU, ECUADOR, and BOLIVIA?

91. What is the name of the sea that is bordering Jordan to the east, and Israel to the west?

92. What is the name of the Forest with a wooded mountain range in Baden-Württemberg, southwestern Germany?

93. What is the name of the valley located on the southern border of Utah with northern Arizona, near the Four Corners area?

94. What is the name of the National Monument in the northern Chihuahuan Desert in the U.S. state of New Mexico?

95. The Lake District is located in which country?

96. The Blue Lagoon is located in which country?

97. Jeju Island is located in which country?

98. Mount Rainier is located in which country?

99. Mackenzie Basin is located in which country?

100. Stone Mountain is located in which country?

101. What is the name of the zoo located in southeastern Muskingum County, Ohio United States?

102. In which country is the second largest zoo in the world by area called Sri Venkateswara zoological park located?

103. What is the name of one of the oldest zoos in the United States located in Virginia, United States?

104. Which country is Living Desert Zoo and Gardens located in?

105. Which country is Arignar Anna Zoological Park located in?

106. What is the name of the largest zoo in Canada located in Toronto, Ontario, Canada?

107. The Pretoria Zoo is located in which country?

108. What is the name of the oldest zoo in Germany and the largest zoo in the world as per the number of animals?

50 Country's Independence Trivia Questions

1. Which country did Algeria gain independence from in the year 1962?

2. How many countries were under the Soviet Union?

3. Which countries in Africa were never colonized?

4. Which year did Argentina gain independence from Spanish Empire?

5. Which country did The Bahamas gain independence from?

6. Which year did Belarus gain independence from the Soviet Union?

7. Which country did Bangladesh gain independence from?

8. Brazil gained independence from the United Kingdom of Portugal, Brazil, and the Algarves in which year?

9. Which year did Canada gain independence from the United Kingdom?

10. Which country colonized Cape Verde?

11. What is the name of Canada's independence day?

12. Which year did Costa Rica gain independence from Spanish Empire?

13. Which country did Croatia gain independence from in 1990?

14. Cuba gained independence from Spanish Empire and which other country?

15. Which country colonized Egypt?

16. Finland gained their independence from the Russian Soviet Federative Socialist Republic in which year?

17. Which year did German reunification happen?

18. 3 October is a day set to commemorate German reunification in Germany, what is that day called?

19. Which empire did Greece gain its independence from?

20. Which country colonized Ghana?

21. Which country colonized Haiti?

22. Which year was Hungary's sovereignty restored after the withdrawal of Soviet troops?

23. Which country did Iceland gain independence from?

24. Which country did India gain independence from in 1947?

25. Which 2 countries did Indonesia gain independence from in 1945?

26. Which year did Iran officially become an Islamic republic after holding a referendum?

27. Which country colonized Iraq?

28. The Declaration of Israel's Independence happen in which year?

29. Which country colonized Jamaica?

30. Which country did North Korea gain independence from in 1948?

31. The Liberation of South Korea from the Empire of Japan happen in which year?

32. Which country colonized Kuwait?

33. Which country colonized Madagascar?

34. Which empire did Mexico gain its independence from in 1810?

35. Nigeria was colonized by the United Kingdom, which country colonized Niger?

36. Which country did Norway gain independence from in 1905?

37. Which country did Pakistan gain independence from in 1947?

38. How many countries made up Yugoslavia?

39. Which country did the Philippines gained independence from in 1946?

40. Which country did Qatar gain independence from in 1971?

41. Which country did Rwanda gain independence from in 1962?

42. Was Serbia under Ottoman Empire or Spanish Empire?

43. Which year did Singapore separate from Malaysia?

44. Which country colonized Malaysia?

45. Which country did Syria gain independence from in 1946?

46. Which year did Tunisia gain independence from France?

47. Which country did the United Arab Emirates gain independence from in 1971?

48. Which year did the United States gain independence from the Kingdom of Great Britain?

49. Which year did Vatican City gain independence from Italy?

50. Which 2 countries did Vietnam gain independence from in 1945?

66 Famous People Trivia Questions

1. What is the nationality of the popular singer Céline Dion?

2. What is the country of origin of the rock band U2 formed in 1976?

3. What is the nationality of the popular talk show host and television producer, Oprah Winfrey?

4. What is the nationality of the popular former basketball player, Michael Jordan?

5. What is the country of origin of the popular singer and songwriter, Paul McCartney?

6. What is the country of origin of the popular singer, pianist, and composer, Elton John?

7. What is the country of origin of the popular filmmaker James Cameron?

8. What is the country of origin of the popular Musician Justin Bieber?

9. What is the country of origin of the popular Musician Rihanna?

10. What is the country of origin of former professional boxer Manny Pacquiao, nicknamed "PacMan"?

11. The popular football player Cristiano Ronaldo is from which country?

12. What is the country of origin of the singer and songwriter Adele?

13. The popular football player Lionel Messi is from which country?

14. Which country is the popular musician Drake from?

15. The popular basketball player LeBron James is from which country?

16. The popular football player Neymar is from which country?

17. The boxer popularly known as Canelo Álvarez or Saúl Álvarez is from which country?

18. The popular tennis player Roger Federer is from which country?

19. The popular football player James Rodriguez is from which country?

20. The popular tennis player Rafael Nadal is from which country?

21. The popular golf player Phil Mickelson is from which country?

22. The popular cricket player MS Dhoni is from which country?

23. The popular runner Usain Bolt is from which country?

24. The popular tennis player Novak Djokovic is from which country?

25. The popular football player Wayne Rooney is from which country?

26. The popular tennis player Maria Sharapova is from which country?

27. The popular golf player Rory McIlroy is from which country?

28. The popular football player Zlatan Ibrahimovic is from which country?

29. What is the country of origin of the comedian, actor, and filmmaker known by the stage name Cantinflas?

30. Which country did Fidel Castro lead from 1959 to 2008?

31. What is the country of origin of the rapper, musician, and actor Wyclef Jean?

32. Nelson Mandela served as the first president of which country from 1994 to 1999?

33. What is the country of origin of the rapper, singer, songwriter, and actor, known professionally as Daddy Yankee?

34. Winston Churchill served as Prime Minister of which country from 1940 to 1945?

35. The human rights activist, feminist, and Nobel Peace Prize laureate, Rigoberta Menchu is from which country?

36. Mahatma Gandhi was an anti-colonial nationalist and political ethicist from which country?

37. The popular singer Shakira, is from which country?

38. Mother Teresa, also known as Saint Teresa of Calcutta is from of which country?

39. The powerful leader in South America Simón José, nicknamed "The Liberator" is from which current day country?

40. Christopher Columbus, the explorer, and navigator who completed four Spanish-based voyages across the Atlantic Ocean from which country?

41. The former professional footballer known as Pelé is from which country?

42. Which country is the father of evolution Charles Darwin from?

43. The explorer and the first European to reach India by sea Vasco da Gama is an origin of which country?

44. One of the greatest and most influential physicists of all time Albert Einstein is a national of which country?

45. The military and political leader Napoleon Bonaparte is a national of which country?

46. Pope John Paul II, the head of the Catholic Church from 1978 until his death in 2005 is from which country?

47. The actor, martial artist, and filmmaker Jean-Claude Van Damme are from which country?

48. The popular painter and scientist Leonardo da Vinci was a citizen of which country?

49. The famous painter Vincent Van Gogh was born in which present-day country?

50. The famous playwright, poet, and actor William Shakespeare was born in which country?

51. The actor, film producer, businessman, former bodybuilder, and politician Arnold Schwarzenegger was born in which country?

52. What is the country of origin of the inventor Thomas Edison?

53. Adolf Hitler was given born in which country?

54. What country was Eric Arthur Blair, known by his pen name George Orwell gave born in which country?

55. The chemist who conducted pioneering research on radioactivity Marie Curie was a citizen of which country?

56. Which country was Elon Musk given birth in?

57. Cleopatra was the queen of which current-day country?

58. Which country was Saddam Hussein president of from 16 July 1979 until 9 April 2003?

59. Margaret Thatcher was Prime Minister of which country from 1979 to 1990?

60. The theoretical physicist, cosmologist, and author Stephen Hawking was a citizen of which country?

61. The former owner of Chelsea Roman Abramovich is a citizen of which country?

62. Which country was prophet Muhammad born in?

63. The popular African football Samuel Etoo is from which country?

64. The founder of the Islamic militant organization al-Qaeda Osama Bin Laden, was given birth to in which country?

65. The popular African football Didier Drogba is from which country?

66. Muammar Gaddafi was a leader of which country?

Answers to Cities of the world

Trivia Questions

1. Thailand

2. United Arab Emirates

3. Malaysia

4. Turkey

5. China

6. India

7. Italy

8. Thailand

9. Taiwan

10. Saudi Arabia

11. Czech Republic

12. South Korea

13. Netherlands

14. Japan

15. Spain

16. Italy

17. Austria

18. Mexico

19. United States

20. Italy

21. Vietnam

22. Canada

23. South Africa

24. Australia

25. Germany

26. Russia

27. Belgium

28. Malaysia

29. Canada

30. Poland

31. Philippines

32. New Zealand

33. Israel

34. France

35. Portugal

36. Brazil

37. Switzerland

38. United Kingdom

39. South Africa

40. Switzerland

41. Morocco

42. Nigeria

43. Ghana

44. Democratic Republic of the Congo

45. Egypt

46. Cameroon

47. Ghana

48. Uganda

49. Senegal

50. Sierra Leone

51. Mozambique

52. Benin

53. Bangladesh

54. China

55. Iraq

56. Saudi Arabia

57. Brazil

58. Venezuela

59. Colombia

60. Venezuela

Answers to Language Trivia Questions

1. Albanian

2. French

3. German

4. English

5. English

6. Yes

7. India

8. Mexico

9. United States

10. Portuguese

11. Bulgarian

12. Spanish

13. Brazil

14. Kazakhstan

15. Pakistan

16. India

17. Northern Cyprus

18. South Korea

19. the Democratic Republic of the Congo

20. Austria

21. Indonesia

22. Albania

23. Egypt

24. Saudi Arabia

25. Iran

26. Nigeria

27. Equatorial Guinea

28. India

29. Nigeria

30. Poland

31. The Netherlands

32. Spanish

33. English

34. Scots

35. Moldova

36. Turkey

37. Cyprus

38. the United States

39. Portuguese

40. The Netherlands

41. Spanish

42. Spanish

43. Danish

44. English

45. Arabic

46. French

47. English

48. Spanish

49. Hungarian

50. Icelandic

51. Hindi

52. Swedish

53. Georgian

54. Russian

55. French

56. English

57. Filipino

58. Arabic

59. Serbian

60. Arabic

Answers to Countries Capitals Trivia Questions

1. Abu Dhabi

2. Ethiopia

3. Netherlands

4. Ankara

5. Athens

6. Baghdad

7. Bangkok

8. Beirut

9. Beijing

10. Berlin

11. Cape Town

12. Brasília

13. Barbados

14. Brussels

15. Hungary

16. Argentina

17. Cairo

18. Australia

19. Caracas

20. Sri Lanka

21. Copenhagen

22. Dakar

23. Syria

24. Bangladesh

25. Qatar

26. Ireland

27. Sierra Leone

28. Georgetown

29. Guatemala City

30. Hanoi

31. Cuba

32. Helsinki

33. Pakistan

34. Jerusalem

35. Kabul

36. Uganda

37. Jakarta

38. Kigali

39. Kingston

40. Kuwait City

41. Kyiv

42. Peru

43. Lisbon

44. London

45. Zambia

46. Luxembourg

47. Madrid

48. Maldives

49. Mexico City

50. Minsk

51. Monaco

52. Moscow

53. Oman

54. Nairobi

55. New Delhi

56. Oslo

57. Ottawa

58. Panama City

59. Paris

60. Port Louis

61. Rabat

62. Riyadh

63. Rome

64. San José

65. San Juan

66. Seoul

67. Singapore

68. Stockholm

69. Taipei

70. Tehran

71. Tokyo

72. Tunis

73. Valletta

74. Victoria

75. Vienna

76. Warsaw

77. Wellington

78. Washington, D.C.

79. Zagreb

80. Abuja

Answers to Currency Trivia Questions

1. Pound Sterling.

2. Tunisian Dinar

3. 10 cents of a US dollar.

4. Kuwaiti Dinar

5. Hungarian forint

6. Venezuelan Bolivar Fuerte

7. Peruvian Sol

8. AFN

9. 1.

10. EUR

11. INR

12. Canada.

13. AUD

14. ZAR

15. NZD

16. USD

17. GBP

18. Julius Caesar.

19. Algerian Dinar

20. Argentine Peso

21. Australian Dollar

22. Euro

23. Bahamian Dollar

24. Taka

25. BYN

26. Euro

27. Indian Rupee

28. Brazilian Real

29. BIF

30. CAD

31. XCD

32. $1.

33. XAF

34. CNY

35. Unidad de Valor Real

36. Costa Rican Colon

37. Kuna

38. Abraham Lincoln.

39. Peso Convertible

40. Danish Krone

41. Dominican Peso

42. US Dollar

43. Egyptian Pound

44. El Salvador Colon

45. Euro

46. Ethiopian Birr

47. Fiji Dollar

48. Euro

49. Euro

50. The $10,000 bill.

51. Ghana Cedi

52. Danish Krone

53. East Caribbean Dollar

54. Gourde

55. Forint

56. Hong Kong Dollar

57. Iceland Krona

58. US Dollar.

59. Indian Rupee

60. Rupiah

61. Iranian Rial

62. Euro

63. Israeli new shekel

64. Jamaican Dollar

65. JPY

66. Kenyan Shilling

67. Kuwaiti Dinar

68. 1,000.

69. Won

70. Lebanese Pound

71. Libyan Dinar

72. CHF

73. Euro

74. Mexican Unidad de Inversion (UDI)

75. Moroccan Dirham

76. Euro

77. New Zealand Dollar

78. Naira

79. Norwegian Krone

80. Pakistan Rupee

81. Balboa

82. Philippine Peso

83. Polish złoty

84. Euro

85. Qatari Rial

86. RUB

87. Rwanda Franc

88. Serbian Dinar

89. Singapore Dollar

90. Euro

91. Rand

92. Euro

93. Swedish Krona

94. WIR Euro

95. Syrian Pound

96. New Taiwan Dollar

97. Baht

98. Turkish Lira

99. Hryvnia

100. UAE Dirham

101. Bolivar

102. Zimbabwe Dollar

103. Brazil Real

104. China Yuan Renminbi and Japan Yen

105. Costa Rica Colon

106. Croatia Kuna

107. All Peso eg. Cuba Peso, Philippines Peso

108. Switzerland Franc

109. Dominican Republic Peso

110. Euro

111. Turkey Lira

112. Hungary Forint

113. India Rupee

114. Russia Ruble

115. Israel Shekel

116. Jamaica Dollar

117. Korea (South and North) Won

118. Nigeria Naira

119. Peru Sol

120. Poland Zloty

Answers to Airlines Trivia

Questions

1. United Arab Emirates

2. Qatar Airways

3. Saudia

4. Malaysia

5. Air New Zealand

6. Japan

7. South Korea

8. China

9. the Philippines

10. the Republic of China (Taiwan)

11. India

12. Australia

13. India

14. Indonesia

15. Malaysia Airlines

16. British Airways

17. United States

18. Singapore Airlines (SIA)

19. Australia

20. United Kingdom

21. Aeroflot

22. Air France

23. United Kingdom

24. Germany

25. Norway

26. Ireland

27. Switzerland

28. Turkish Airlines

29. Spain

30. Air Canada

31. United States

32. Canada

33. Ethiopian Airlines

34. South African Airways (SAA)

35. Air Seychelles

36. Rwandair

37. United Kingdom

38. the Netherlands

39. Finland

40. the United Arab Emirates

Answers to Brands Trivia

Questions

1. Germany

2. Japan

3. USA

4. France

5. Italy

6. Japan

7. Germany

8. South Korea

9. Italy

10. France

11. France

12. Germany

13. Germany

14. Italy

15. Switzerland

16. France

17. USA

18. Switzerland

19. United Kingdom

20. Italy

21. Japan

22. United Kingdom

23. Italy

24. France

25. Italy

26. China

27. United Kingdom

28. South Korea

29. Italy

30. Germany

31. USA

32. USA

33. USA

34. USA

35. Austria

36. United States

37. Netherlands

38. Sweden

39. China

40. USA

41. Japan

42. Japan

43. USA

44. South Korea

45. Italy

46. Germany

47. United States

48. United States

49. Switzerland

50. United States

51. Russia

52. United States

53. Switzerland

54. United States

55. United States

Answers to Countries slogan

Trivia Questions

1. Ukraine

2. Israel

3. El Salvador

4. El Salvador

5. the Netherlands

6. United Kingdom

7. Japan

8. France

9. United States

10. Thailand

11. Nepal

12. Hong Kong, Taiwan, Singapore, and South Korea.

13. Cuba

14. A city in the United States named Los Angeles

15. The "city of gold" is Johannesburg in South Africa

16. Belgium

17. Brazil

18. India

19. Zambia

20. Finland

21. Bangladesh

22. Denmark

23. Germany

24. Libya

25. Rome

26. Ireland

27. Nigeria

28. Egypt

29. Kerala, India

30. Ghana

31. India

32. Afghanistan

33. Afghanistan

34. Switzerland

35. Bahrain

36. Scotland

37. Bangladesh

38. Australia

39. Norway

40. Thailand

41. boltBhutan

42. Singapore

43. England

44. Sri Lanka

45. India

46. Switzerland

47. South Africa

48. China

49. Vietnam

50. Ancient Greek

51. North Korea

52. Australia

53. South Korea

54. Palestine

55. Uganda

56. The United States

57. Belarus

58. United kingdom

59. Iceland

60. Albania

61. Bulgaria

62. Croatia

63. Germany

64. Italy

65. Monaco

66. Montenegro

67. Slovenia

68. Indonesia

69. Philippines

70. Saudi Arabia

71. Turkey

72. United Arab Emirates (UAE)

73. Canada

74. Panama

75. United States of America (USA)

76. Colombia

77. Venezuela

78. New Zealand

79. Lesotho

80. Burkina Faso

Answers to Countries Motto Trivia Questions

1. Order and progress

2. Freedom and order

3. From sea to sea

4. Fatherland or death

5. Justice, Peace, Work

6. God, King, and Fatherland

7. God, Fatherland, Liberty

8. United in diversity

9. France

10. Unity and justice and freedom

11. Freedom or Death

12. Liberty, equality, fraternity

13. With the help of God for Homeland and Freedom

14. Truth alone triumphs

15. God is the Greatest

16. Ireland forever

17. Out of Many, One People

18. Strength and consistency

19. The Homeland is First

20. God, the Country, the King

21. I will maintain

22. Onward

23. Unity and Faith, Peace and Progress

24. Everything for Norway

25. Faith, unity, discipline

26. God, Honour, Homeland

27. There is no God other than God and Muhammad is the Messenger of God

28. Further beyond

29. One for all, all for one

30. God and my right

Answers to Citizens Trivia

Questions

1. a Finn

2. Australians

3. a Bangladeshi

4. Belarusians or Belarusans

5. Belgium

6. a Tswana

7. a Briton

8. Brazilians

9. Canadians

10. Chinese

11. Chileans

12. Republic of Congo

13. Croatia

14. Cubans

15. Cyprus

16. Czech

17. a Dane

18. Ecuadoreans

19. Salvadoreans

20. Egypt

21. Ethiopians

22. a Frenchwoman

23. Gabonese

24. Georgians

25. Germans

26. Ghanaians

27. Greeks

28. a Haitian

29. Dutch

30. Hungarians

31. an Icelander

32. Indians

33. Indonesians

34. Iraqi

35. an Irishman or an Irishwoman

36. Israelis

37. Italians

38. Jamaicans

39. Japanese

40. Kazakhs

41. Kuwaiti

42. Lebanese

43. a Luxembourger

44. Kuwaiti

45. a Malagasy

46. Malaysians

47. Maltese

48. Mexicans

49. a Monégasque

50. Mozambicans

51. Nepalese

52. a Netherlander

53. New Zealand

54. Nigerien

55. North Koreans

56. Norwegians

57. Pakistanis

58. Peruvians

59. a Filipino

60. a Pole

61. Portuguese

62. Qatari

63. Russian

64. a Saudi

65. a Scot

66. Senegalese

67. Serb

68. Seychellois

69. Singaporeans

70. Slovak

71. a Slovene

72. a Spaniard

73. Sudanese

74. a Swede

75. Swiss

76. Taiwanese

77. Thai

78. Togolese

79. a Turk

80. Ukrainians

81. Emirati

82. a US citizen

83. Vietnamese

84. Welsh

85. Yemeni

Answers to Countries

Landmarks Trivia Questions

1. New York, United States

2. Paris, France.

3. China

4. Russia

5. Moscow, Russia.

6. Saudi Arabia

7. Italy

8. Egypt

9. Australia

10. India

11. Peru

12. London, UK

13. Rome, Italy

14. the United States

15. the United States

16. Japan

17. Vatican City

18. Paris, France

19. Germany

20. United Kingdom

21. Tanzania

22. Australia

23. Egypt

24. United Kingdom

25. China

26. China–Nepal

27. United States

28. Dubai, United Arab Emirates

29. Athens, Greece

30. Venice, Italy

31. United States

32. United Kingdom

33. France

34. Bavaria, Germany

35. Switzerland

36. Italy

37. Italy

38. United Kingdom

39. Peru

40. Canada

41. United States

42. the United States and Canada

43. Dubai, United Arab Emirates

44. France

45. United States

46. Kuala Lumpur, Malaysia

47. United Kingdom

48. United States

49. Japan

50. Italy

51. Italy

52. United States

53. British overseas territory

54. United States

55. United States

56. United Kingdom

57. United Kingdom

58. Egypt

59. Berlin, Germany

60. United States

61. Italy

62. Mexico

63. Zimbabwe and Zambia

64. China

65. China

66. China

67. Florence, Italy

68. Israel

69. Beijing, China

70. Island of Sicily, Italy.

71. Japan

72. United States

73. Paris France

74. Netherlands

75. Russia

76. Finland

77. Copenhagen, Denmark

78. Northern Ireland

79. France

80. South Africa

81. Russia

82. United States

83. Istanbul, Turkey

84. India

85. Australia

86. Brazil

87. United States

88. New Zealand

89. Australia

90. Amazon Rainforest

91. The Dead Sea

92. The Black Forest

93. Monument Valley

94. White Sands

95. United Kingdom

96. Iceland

97. South Korea

99. New Zealand

100. Georgia

101. The Wilds

102. India

103. Smithsonian National Zoological Park

104. United States

105. India

106. Toronto Zoo

107. South Africa

108. Berlin Zoological Garden

Answers to Country's independence Trivia Questions

1. France

2. 15

3. Ethiopia and Liberia

4. 9 July 1816

5. United Kingdom

6. 1991

7. Pakistan

8. 1822

9. 1867

10. Portugal

11. Canada Day

12. 1821

13. SFR Yugoslavia

14. United States

15. United Kingdom

16. 1917

17. 1990

18. German Unity Day

19. Ottoman Empire

20. United Kingdom

21. France

22. 1991

23. Denmark

24. United Kingdom

25. Netherlands and Japan

26. 1979

27. United Kingdom

28. 14 May 1948

29. United Kingdom

30. Soviet Union

31. 1945

32. United Kingdom

33. France

34. Spanish Empire

35. France

36. Sweden

37. United Kingdom

38. 6 republics

39. United States

40. United Kingdom

41. Belgium

42. Ottoman Empire

43. 1965

44. United Kingdom

45. France

46. 1956

47. United Kingdom

48. 1776

49. 1929

50. Empire of Japan and France

Answers to Famous People

Trivia Questions

1. Canadian

2. Ireland

3. American

4. American

5. United Kingdom

6. United Kingdom

7. Canadian

8. Canadian

9. Barbados

10. Philippines

11. Portugal

12. United Kingdom

13. Argentina

14. Canadian

15. United States

16. Brazil

17. Mexico

18. Switzerland

19. Colombia

20. Spain

21. United States

22. India

23. Jamaica

24. Serbia

25. United Kingdom

26. Russia

27. Northern Ireland

28. Sweden

29. Mexico

30. Cuba

31. Haiti

32. South Africa

33. Puerto Rico

34. The United Kingdom

35. Guatemala

36. India

37. Colombia

38. India

39. Venezuela

40. Italy

41. Brazil

42. United Kingdom

43. Portugal

44. Germany

45. France

46. Poland

47. Belgian

48. Italy

49. Netherlands

50. United Kingdom

51. Austria

52. United States

53. Austria

54. India

55. Poland

56. South Africa

57. Egypt

58. Iraq

59. United Kingdom

60. United Kingdom

61. Russia

62. Saudi Arabia

63. Cameroon

64. Saudi Arabia

65. Ivory Coast

66. Libya

29424680R00066